Poems by
Fleda Brown Jackson

Purdue University Press
West Lafayette, Indiana

Library of Congress Cataloging-in-Publication Data

Jackson, Fleda Brown, 1944-
    Fishing with blood: poems / by Fleda Brown Jackson.
        p.   cm.
    ISBN 0–911198–94–6 (pbk.)
    I. Title.
PS3560.A21534F5 1988   87-32460
811'.54—dc19   CIP

Printed in the United States of America

For Dennis
And for Jeanne Murray Walker

CONTENTS

I

II

III

IV

ACKNOWLEDGMENTS

Grateful acknowledgment is made to the following publications in which some of the poems in this volume first appeared: *Ariel:* "Emily Dickinson's Love"; *Beloit Poetry Journal:* "Arch," "Edward Hopper's Woman," and "Rabbits"; *Cedar Rock:* "Goat"; *The Crescent Review:* "Bed-Buffaloes, Nose-Fairies, Car-Key Gnomes"; *Croton Review:* "Living in Grandfather's House" and "A Plain Philosophical Choice"; *DeKalb Literary Arts Journal:* "Home of the Razorbacks"; *Indiana Review:* "Apalachee Bay" and "Celebrating Your Fortieth Birthday with Conway Twitty"; *Iowa Review:* "Maintenance"; *The Mickle Street Review:* "Chicken Willie"; *Mid-American Review:* "Catching Turtles" and "He Gives Me Some Idea of Why He Is the Way He Is" (originally titled "To Give You Some Idea of Why I Am the Way I Am"); *Midwest Quarterly:* "Sky Watch"; *The Poet:* "Daughter, You Step Through Me"; *Poetry Northwest:* "The Catch," "Fishing with Blood" (originally titled "Family Chronicles"), and "Saving a Life"; *The Poetry Review:* "Keeping Fit"; *Southern Humanities Review:* "To Mark, My Retarded Brother, Who Lived 20 Years and Learned to Speak 300 Words" (in Vol. 15); *Sou'wester:* "In Delaware, the Winters Are Milder"; and *Yarrow:* "Breaking the Dark," "Devil's Den," "Plain People," and "Small Inheritances."

Acknowledgment is also made for permission to reprint the following: "A Mother Watches Her Athletic Daughter"—This work first appeared in the *Cimarron Review* and is reprinted here with the permission of the Board of Regents for Oklahoma State University, holders of the copyright; and "The Scholar's Cat"—First published in *The Kenyon Review*—New Series, Fall 1983, Vol. V, No. 4. Copyright © by Kenyon College. Reprinted with permission of author and publisher.

"Apalachee Bay" and "To Mark, My Retarded Brother, Who Lived 20 Years and Learned to Speak 300 Words" were reprinted in *Anthology of Magazine Verse and Yearbook of American Poetry* (Beverly Hills: Monitor Book Company) in 1985 and 1984, respectively.

The manuscript for this book was completed with the aid of a grant from the Delaware State Arts Council.

As tendrils sometimes fling themselves out from the thicker
bushes, his desire will fling itself out
from the tangle of family and hang there, swaying in the light.

"Duration of Childhood"
Ranier Maria Rilke

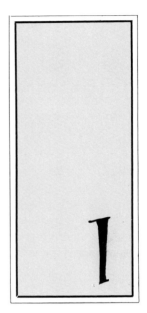

GARDEN

My father is up at 6:30
in his bare chest and pajama bottoms,
whistling among the tomatoes,
brooding over the ruffled petunias
along the driveway wall. I watch him
through the screen door
where the morning has not yet
touched me, thin as a nightgown.
He looks like a circus man, performing
tricks too small for his muscles,
cross-pollinating petunias
with a tiny paintbrush, lifting
away their yellow powder.
Also, he looks like a huge eye
down on the tiny mechanics
of the world. I watch his deliberate
move, his mingling of dust.
My mother is still in bed, soft as clay,
anonymous as sheets. She would get up
and start in on last night's dishes,
if she had the energy.
It seems that we have drawn it out
of her, that the sun is wrong to shine.
Her energy is out there, loose
barefoot in the garden, pajama strings
loose, careless of himself, careful
of the type: the Big Boy tomatoes,
the Hungarian yellow peppers.
He might be no one, in the flesh,
except for his green orchestration,
his rows. He whistles Ode to Joy,
getting it right, yes, this is it,
is it, ties each note on its trellis
like a good child climbing
to heaven. I stick out my tongue
against the bitter screen, to taste
whether I am a woman or a man, and
whose I am, and for what I was made.

WHAT YOUR EYES HAVE TO SEE

1

When the grapevines dried in the jungle
by the house, they drew pure fire.
We crouched by the creek, electric as deer.
We knew how it was done: raise your chin,
hold smoke behind your lips like a woman
on the waterfront, drunk with smoke
and hard enough to take the rest of her life
as it comes. You want it to look easy.
You want to open your mouth
and let "no comment" curl up, stinging
like the steam of infidels between
your eyes and what your eyes have to see.

2

What my eyes had to see was a plain chicken
killed by our landlord Mr. Hankins, as if
this were the Middle Ages. I climbed up
from the creek too late for the moment
of the neck, but soon enough for the pitching
and slinging of blood on the grass,
blood-eyes flying at the sky, a dream of blood
stronger than houses or modern plumbing
or churches. I saw this, miserable with happiness,
blessed. Nothing is closer than death,
wrung out, bled dry, the ecstasy of lifting off
and letting go, petulant as feathers.

3

Deader than dead, dried, pickled, or at least
the rumor of it: a dead man lay blatant
as an open door, stretched out to study
at the university, in Fine Arts. All his parts
took the sun through a green windowshade.
He was all there, his limbs and stomach
laid out absolutely sure of themselves,
the head shriveled to little significance,
lips drawn in a helpless grin. We said
to touch the face was death, but it was only
the face of the old cold rumor, so lonely
we quit believing anything we saw.

SKY WATCH

1

Down front at the drive-in
before the show starts, my sister
and I ride the merry-go-round
through the dust with steely grip,
leaning to watch the sky whirl
pink. When both my feet land
solid on the grass,
the evening star still falls
through my eyes, out of control.
The screen starts pale movements;
the voice over our heads
hugely announces.
I take my little sister's hand.
Before me, rows and rows of cars,
turning one color in the dusk.
The same hollow voice suggesting
hot dogs, popcorn, into every window.
The screen, coming up brighter and
brighter like a space craft landing.

2

The Big Bang cannon belongs
to my father and his brother
from the old days. Once a summer,
at dusk, he sets it on the dock
and fires a wooden plug over the lake,
claiming he can see it hit the water,
somewhere. Get your mother,
he says, hunkered clumsy
as Gulliver over the toy,
funneling in gunpowder, traveling
back with its acrid ghost.
We know the old days were cast iron
and lead, because he has also
shown us soldiers, melted
to a shining, re-formed, melted,
throwing off burdens again and again.
Tell your mother, he says,
to come out and watch me
before the sky is dark as pitch.

5

3

I climb the willow to watch
aurora borealis play over the black
lake. My cousin is a breath
from my cheek, straddling limbs.
I have a game, pretend to jump:
suicide is the word I say
for his arm to hold me back.
His arm is a stranger,
and the thought of his arm
is stranger than my life
to this point. I am shiftier
than the sky, transformed to a tragic
case, needing a kiss. I kiss him,
then, straight on the night's mouth.
Already, the huge sky closes down.
And the slow trees that used
to branch any way in the world.

4

Halley's comet arrives hazy
over Michigan, Missouri, and Texas.
People I love in those places
plan to watch, but forget.
Over their heads, the snowball
rages toward the sun, trailing
30 million miles of hairy
luminescence, flips its hair
over its shoulder and backs off
through Taurus and Capricorn.
Goodby for 75 years.
I change phone companies
while there's time, trying
to clear up the fuzz and fade
of voices. Only last night,
I shouted to my mother three times:
"Yes, the 23rd, by car."
The old loneliness, making promises.
I circle grief and joy
like a star in the East.

TO MARK, MY RETARDED BROTHER, WHO LIVED 20 YEARS AND LEARNED TO SPEAK 300 WORDS

Nobody has any business but me, to tell how
you came home, a white ball up pitted concrete steps,
home to our grandmother's swirled carpet.
Knitted bundle, you wailed clues of that soft
rotten, that misconnection, that sever, that spasm
which broke your mother's heart into blank starts.
You drug your feet, child.

Across the wood floor your twirling walker,
the rattling dance lurched down
fourteen steps: you were never lucky.
Your spilled blood flowed like menses, expected
rupture, bombardment of corners, ridges, juts.
The red record player sat on the chest
by the window. I don't remember it new:
blood, spit, and dirt where you plied
that delicate spinning with your scratched hands.
"Getting to know you," know you, you and
Deborah Kerr on the vowels, one long happy drool.
Hollyhock ladies on the sill, I lined up for you.
With a towel, I held that white head
which smashed into the blank floor
and everything, I think, I could ever know.
You grew to be a white crane, your head
bobbling on the tops of your friends
who took you to play with perfect aplomb.
Little citizens already, in the grass,
they calculated games you could not wreck.
I was the one who ran barefoot, terror light
to grab you loping onto Garland Street,
laughing. I could have bashed in your head,
unsubtle brother, smiling outline.
Angel face, pushing to break with rudiments,
the best word for you is unused.

So your ankles drew up solemnly,
wrists in. The spasm locked. When I came to you
in your sterile steel circus, the last clowns
had gone home. Malicious beard raked your face.
On your head, practical blonde hair razed
at short attention.
You seemed so heavy you would never float away.
Then you sank into your coffin in flannel pajamas,
the warmest bed you ever felt.

ARCH

Every day she walked to school through
the wet grass and along the confusion
of steel, rising to be the new field house.
Every day she walked home, stopping to watch
the huge arches flash with welders,
and men yell instructions across the beams.

"It was an ordinary Wednesday afternoon,"
she would say after that, although
it became ordinary only when something happened
to measure it by.

She had crossed the field to Terry Village
where her mother was hanging diapers
on the line and her brother was throwing toys
off his blue quilt. She was standing
on the porch eating a fig newton
when she happened to look up and see
the great arch lean and the tiny body drop,
in slow-motion, like all catastrophe.

She remembered the little arms waving,
the tremor when the steel struck,
and the dust rising like smoke.
She imagined the body, final
as a bag of sand. She thought of the workman
that morning, buttoning a khaki shirt,
leaving for work, lighting a Lucky Strike
on his way out the door, telling someone goodby.
She thought of the omens in a regular day,
the arch she walked under ten minutes ago.
She felt like an angel, transcending events.
She thought which muscles she might have tried
if she had been the workman, suddenly needing to fly.

I LEAPT OVER THE WALL

That summer my grandmother gave me
her Reader's Digest Condensed Books
because I was thirteen and ready
for the essence without the whole weight.

I read late into the morning heat,
elegant in bed with oranges and tea:
three times, especially, the story
of the nun, her bliss
as the sisters sheared
her rampaging hair, bruised
her knees on the stones
of her cell. She fell
into papery silence

which seemed to me like love—
to start each day knowing
who to be in the habit of,
black and white,
bell and clapper,
infatuation all day
like a caught dove beating
faint breasts awake.

Elaborate love
took such prayer
of knees, of hands,
of wretched sinner hands
lost in the summer sheets
looking for the way
spirit reaches flesh.

So close, but at the end,
the nun folded her robes for good.
Outside the convent wall,
rain dropped a chaos of tears
on her complicated hair.

Inside, the disappointed sisters
gathered up their beads
to bring the whole weight of the Father
upon them like grapes into wine.

LIVING IN GRANDFATHER'S HOUSE

While Grandfather was off preaching
the Single Tax to save the poor,
we moved into his house on Garth Avenue.
Downstairs, his bevelled windows laid
elegant rainbows on the rug
where we scattered our dolls, pennies,
records, and panties like heathens.
The real ivory piano keys peeled off
to a beggar's grin.

Then Aunt Cleone and her boys moved in.
At this time, I learned the importance
of private ownership and free enterprise.
Soon, my mother was measuring the rice
and counting bread. Around the table,
she ladled half-cups of stew,
three-fourths of milk. Cousin Alan
wanted the steakbone marrow.
so it came to a vote.

Under communism, nothing belongs to you.
When I lay in bed with my Monday stomach,
Aunt Cleone took her shoulders in the door
to tell me she knew my game.
Even my father drifted off to the park,
flying planes with the boys.

At the university, his father's friends
hurried him toward his father's degree,
but in his father's basement,
he whittled exact propellers.
At dinner he lectured on torque and lift
and other theories of freedom.

FOR GRANDMOTHER BETH

Just one scandalous year past our
grandmother's death, the second wife
stood homely and trembling ankle-deep
in the lake, taking on water and family at
once. Once, she told me, your grandfather
found the box of hair your grandmother
saved when she had it bobbed. She said
he cried, and I tried to imagine both
wives working it out in heaven. He took
this second one, taught her theories of
economics, gave her his grown children
and grandchildren, money and houses. They
used to sit at the kitchen table and eat
prunes, the same table where he ate
prunes with my grandmother. Regularity
took him to ninety-five, although
the last year in the nursing home he
couldn't remember who she was, and even
years before that, at the lake, he'd
call her by his dead wife's name. No,
Harry, she'd say, it's Beth, Beth, and
lead him back to where he meant to
go. She never touched the money he left
her, saved it for his children, took
in roomers and lived on interest. Now
she's dead and all Garth Avenue is
gone from me, from us, the house, the
lilies-of-the-valley on the north
side, oh, it would be a long list, and
who cares now but us. This is what I
have to say for her, who held a place
and saved everything as if she had no
needs, or wishes, except to be no
trouble at all, and to die quickly, a
light turned out to save electric bills.

A Plain Philosophical Choice

Blake Jett in his stripped-down Ford
could roar off with the loose girls. We
walked, cradling western civilization
in hardback against our breasts.
We were the smart track and we knew it.
In gym class and homeroom, they mixed
everything up like democracy,
but we knew their signs.
We gave them blue ink, wide
margins, engravable words.

But one by one, we came into our hormones,
plebian as Kotex. Under our skirts,
the bulge of equipment, buried like sin.
Voluminous notes were exchanged on the matter.
Nina Spalding's tight skirts risked
as much as our parents warned, and
overnight, she was gone, with her stomach.
Ricky and Elvis conflicted down our bulletin boards,
a plain philosophical choice: country-club white,
or the deep rumble from the edge of black.

A person could settle for anything.
The school could blow up, the town, the U.S.A.
A person could go crazy with waiting.
After school, a person could take a certain bus,
to sit with a certain boy, and leave
her arrogant friends to walk.
Down the hillside,
the ribbon of buses was always numbered.
Inside, their handrails worn to steel,
the wounds of their gray seats picked bare.
Soon the drivers would grind their motors
one after the other
and roll their yellow machines downhill
until they broke away like pollen.

BREAKING THE DARK

The night someone pushed me into the fortuneteller's tent
at the Washington County Fair in Fayetteville, Arkansas,
I already had a plastic fan, a mirror, and a stuffed rabbit.

One expected—what? A gypsy parody in skirts
and shirts, scarves, beads and tinsel, an armory
of rings. So: she was no disappointment, mummified

in color, but she flicked her bangles back like flies,
as if this nonsense only draped the theater to please
the literal fans. She took my hand. I had kept it from her

all my nineteen years, and now must pay.
She closed hers down, massaged my naked palm,
blind, exultant in the flesh. Her fingers traced

the lifeline, touched the scars of vanished warts,
the reddened cuticles: "You will marry young. Children
will come after a long wait. You will travel to the sea."

There was nothing in her grab-bag spiel, but
the fright of darkness took me in, the secret
rumored words, the white hands witching, finding out

my carbon self, gathering evidence. Then she was gone.
The dark physics of the Tilt-a-Whirl, so whisked up
in lights, came clean as picked bones to the shock of day.

—I can prove these are not the hands I started with.
Now they divide and subdivide by complicated lines;
bones rise up, veins shadow toward my fingertips.

These hands grow garish, gypsy-like. They take
the firefly hints that pulse the dark and make them
prophesy for strangers, a code to break the dark.

PIANO

My fingers try to remember Blessed Assurance
and Jesus Loves Me, sending Sunday school chords
out the window to an August sky's retreat.

I wish I could honestly play the old paradox,
strike the mathematics of forgiveness and doom
that uncoils the night into God's hands.

Not even believers believe anymore, except
in their blood. C-chords, G-chords, still climb
out of the heart, goading the derelict fingers

to finish a story, any familiar story: the sky
is a dominant arch. In the startled space beneath,
Babel rose to a quandary, shivered, fell flat. All

that stood, we nailed up on the right-angle clash
of good and evil, under the careful wings of angels
flashing the time, the time, out of the corner

of an eye. I try to remember my childhood as
just one still scene, humming with the terrible thing
called love. That pitch, invented again.

SMALL INHERITANCES

To escape the weight of Christmas,
my father takes his slow Pinto
impeccably over the ice
to Cape Rock, so we can hike.
The gate is locked, and my mother
is in our ears, pitching her tones,
laying down the law, but we park
the car and slip along the mile
to the trail, alone and happily
unorthodox. Old leaves break clear
as wind chimes under our feet.

On the pond, frost has grown
leaf-crystals in a symmetry
that brings us to our knees,
focusing our eyes. Below
the surface, another layer
hovers like wings in ice.

"You could drive a truck on this,"
my father says, so we give it all we have,
skating in our boots, scraping
like barbarians through crystal.

We climb to the bluff
along a torrent of ice, catching
our feet on pignuts and leafbeds.
Below us, the Mississippi,
solid, except for one wide curve
lolling through its center,
dragging crusts downstream.
From this height, there is
the stubborn urge to leap,
to fix the boundary in a flash.

On the way back, my father points
to the spots where trillium,
bloodroot, and shooting stars
come up in the spring. And
jack-in-the-pulpits, protected
by a sign. At home, he drags out
his slides, closeup after closeup
of the tiniest blooms, his
favorite subjects, their ornery
faces sharp against the green mist.

CELEBRATING YOUR FORTIETH BIRTHDAY
WITH CONWAY TWITTY

The first chance out, you leave Arkansas
for the articulate East. Then one day
half your probable life is gone
and you are practiced at the wheel.
I-95 eases under your fingers
from Washington to New York:
you tick off rest stops like a grocery list.
Overhead, electric maps are wired
from joint to joint. Electricity collects
in the radio and comes out twenty-five years old.
Are you warm, are you real, Mona Lisa,
or just a cold and lonely, lovely work of art?
You choose this sudden artifact to catch up
with yourself. You sing along, losing
half the lyrics. You decide to cry.

You pick the boy at Jug Wheeler's Drive-In
who bought you cherry Cokes and lip synched
the whole hit parade, curling his lip,
believing it himself. You put him in the dark,
grabbing your shoe to keep you on the right side
of the Woodland Cemetery wall. You weren't
supposed to feel him kiss your hair.
Five years later, you heard he pulled a knife
in the Dickson Street Barbershop, got sent
to Bentonville. You hear he is in and out again.

And now you are here, in your Subaru,
giving your hands and feet rational signals.
You feel anemic and cold, a work of art,
and the South becomes your metaphor.
You make it mean the live heat of you.
You make it mean everything you can't say.

In Delaware, the Winters Are Milder

1

Shoving its white sky into place,
day reports in. Newark, Delaware.
Low firs hush against the window.
The only birch, planted dead center of the yard,
grey-white, invisible on the sky,
wraps the phone wires with tiny upper branches.

Beyond the backyards of this subdivision
the train rolls, an undercurrent,
trembling all the windows, cabinet doors, walls.
A peculiar thing, the trembling. There is no sound
or clank of cars. At night, at morning,
an underground motor shakes, a secret riveter works.

At night the streetlight cancels the dark,
a perpetual full moon. Further, high across the tracks,
the car plant casts a pink haze.
We call it Jesus Chrysler.
It never goes out, all night suffuses pink.

2

Back in the Ozark hills winter struck dreadful.
The ground was a rock. Its cold rose like mist
into the floor. We covered the doors with blankets.
Bedrooms shut off from the furnace like tombs,
breathed cold. Sharp blue skies hollowed our bones,
then billowed, greyed, and dumped hailstones,
glazed the roads with ice, left trees
blinding with ice, broken and split.
Deliberate white snow flooded from the sky
like a miracle.

There are people there who live on nothing,
who barely live from heat to heat.
You can hear them in spring, sun suppliants,
yelling at their children who wrestle in the grass,
in yellow crocus, purple hyacinths, and violets.
Violence gets them through.

A Mother Watches Her Athletic Daughter

You make one long spider's pull
down the bluff, rope spinning from your belly
as your mountains grind to plains
with storybook speed.
You plié, absorb the shock.
Your body is a taut bow,
springing and releasing.

I used to watch my mother bent over the tub,
the curve of her back, her breasts
drawing her down like lead.
She would lift them, surprised
and humble as a child, fog them
like a baby's behind with powder.

So I thought I fell at last
out of love with swelling
and shrinking and swelling.
Then you were born,
and your brother. I kept climbing
the narrow stairs where your voices echoed.

Now you rappel on a shaft
of afternoon sunlight
until your shoes crunch
into dry leaves, and the cord
flops loose. I am so still,
hoping you can do it
over and over.

Daughter, You Step through Me

Daughter, you step through me
as easily as glass
breaking. An angel in my skin.

In a swath behind you
all clutter sweeps aside
into the simplest path.

That boy is sheepish to have you
be so pretty in your blue shorts
and blonde skin. You step out

the door as through brocade,
tropic beads, or wisteria blooms.
Now you wheel away, arced

like racers. I could be
a bent crone, collecting chaff
in a field still restless

from your sudden harvest.
I could be the last thought
your final eyes see.

HOME OF THE RAZORBACKS

Homesick again, watching these buds break,
the high breeze spinning one-arm maple wings
like wishes. I feel the Boston Mountains roll
against me with their old soft green breasts.

I take it slow, from Alma, Arkansas, straight up
Highway 71, then bank left into the first curve
and its long pale overlook. I downshift shrewd
as a hillbilly, gauging what I can and can't do.

God relaxes his grip and I am free, climbing
with the expert trailer-trucks, easing from gear
to gear. Off the edge, miles of sweet green haze
are laced with dogwood, but I am holding the road
up Mount Gaylor to the last plateau where half-

hearted tourist shops announce in peeling paint,
"Highest Point in the Ozarks." Arkansas people like
the folds and crevices, so I am flying down the north
side, holding on, slowing into Mountainburg, West Fork.
Then in the dream I am on the edge of Fayetteville,

looking down into its mountainous Razorback heart
the way I want to know myself. It sprawls plush and deep,
jagged with civilization and haphazard streets.
This place is so clear and real it is almost death.
All my life, I have kept leaving it to stay alive.

CENTRAL LAKE

COTTAGE

It is like opening the door
on my grandmother's bones.
By this time,
they have grown vulnerable
as a crust of snow,
almost a fiction, almost
easier than the actual
dust fallen from history
along the rocker, the mantle,
smelling like cedar.
This cottage is nothing
but split trees.
I have come to help hang
screens, scrub floors,
lay out the dock,
pump water, throw
the rowboat into the lake.
Old motions rise out of us
like ghosts, light
enough to go on forever.
Our shadow selves come
dripping up the dock,
track sand across the floor,
play spin-the-bottle
by the fire, trembling
to think whose mouth
the bottle points to, and
what way is best. No sooner
than I lean against the kiss,
the door cracks open
on those melting bones.

OUT BACK

Once I heard an owl
through a tunnel from the moon,
imagined it huge
in its eyes, floating down
from the woods toward the lake.

All things moved down,
the life of trees clawed
at the hill, roots rolled
downhill in rivulets
beneath the lantern.
Behind my back, the cottage
slid toward the water
like an ice cube melting.

"See the eyes of the owl,"
my grandmother said, holding
the lantern to the trees
where something stirred, but
even the eyes had closed
into the awful dark.

My grandmother stood lean
and erect, her hair already loose
for the night and waved down
her back like the real woman
in a fairy tale. She said
my name, which was also her
name, said it out at the night
to make me appear, and hold.

SPROUTS

Aunt Cleone arrives with her home-
ground flour, distilled water,
three loaves of bread, cold-pressed
oil, mung beans, alfalfa seeds,
chick peas, squares of nylon
net, and vitamins.
I take her to buy carrots,
tomatoes, broccoli, and cauliflower
from the local one-eyed
vegetable man, who flatly
refuses to save the malva for her
that grows between his rows.
"I consider that a weed," he says.
She likes to grind it up, for some
good thing it has in it. "Weeds,"
she tells him, "are just plants
in the wrong place."
On top of the cottage woodstove
she rinses and drains seeds
through the net, sets them up
to sprout, to double their worth.
Then she sits upstairs in the lotus
position, in the center of the star
she painted on the floor
when she was twelve.
She looks like her mother
as I knew her: relentlessly
straight, yellowish-gray hair
lasting to her waist.
This place is as close as she can get
to an accurate root down.

IMPLEMENTS

The yellow duck-and-dog bowl,
the bluebird bowl,
the crinkle-glass pitcher,
the Mary Pickford spoon,
the Douglas Fairbanks spoon,
the Charlie McCarthy spoon,
the wooden pail, the aluminum pail,
the big dipper and the little dipper:
I set these things down, each
final, capable of survival
without implications.
Yet they deliver themselves outward
like water rings from water reeds,
until we are carried into our own lives,
like messengers, propelled
from their forms. This year
we tear away the 1960 newsprint
from the kitchen shelves
and stick down blue-plaid Contact paper,
a minor violation, a slicker
footing for the bowls. No one
can remember exactly what's been broken,
or lost, but things are missing,
things are missing,
we can tell from the feel of it.

CANOE

This is how Alan rebuilt
the Thompson Brothers canoe:
He loosened the gunnels,
pulled the tacks
out, unscrewed the keel,
and the old canvas fell away.
He fixed a couple of broken
ribs, set the frame inside
a canvas hammock
pulled with block and tackle.
Inside that, he set
concrete blocks for weight,
and wiggled the frame
for a week until the canvas
loved its shape. He wrapped
and tacked the ends, coated
the canvas with sealer
hard enough to sand.
Then he screwed the gunnels
on, then the brass
at bow and stern, then
the keel. This is how much
love there is in the fingers,
in the shapes given to the eye

when the eye hardly knows
what it sees. The fingers
draw back the shape
of sliding through
the water, of evening
and morning, of coming
along the cusp
of light and dark
with no sound, moving
as if moving were a wish
pulling itself.
The paddle goes down
like muscle, a faint slap.
The shape is the channel,
the ribbed basket,
the lightness of breaking
through, the suspension
between sky and floor,
a sigh, a stretch
of canvas like a drawn
bow, lean as fingers.

BLACKBERRIES

Richie Osborne and Tom Ross
discovered Dave Roberts
about a mile up in the woods
behind the lake
in a one-room red house
papered with magazine pictures
of movie stars and boxers.
They'd listen to his blow-by-blow
of the Joe Louis/Max Schmeling fight
and the last Louis/Marciano fight.
They said it was like
a ringside seat, Old Dave's hair
shaking in his words.
After someone moved his house down
close to the crossroads so he could
pick up his groceries, all of us
used to climb the hills
to the wild blackberries
and bring him a jarful of the hard
and bitter things, since he couldn't
go back that far himself anymore.

WHALER

I teach my niece Elizabeth
to let down her oars,
then pull and lift with mine.
Our wake smooths
like a tail. Elizabeth says
we are a dragonfly,
double-oared. I think
we are an old woman,
our low whaler spreading
the reeds with wide hips,
sloshing hollow.
Elizabeth talks nonsense
about Indians from Moscow
who spray their hair
with Raid. She imagines
molecules, red against
green, jostling the lake
like jello. Sure.
And there were wildcats once
across the road, eating
the Knowles's chickens
and eating the loser of
hide-and-seek, who
would be thrown to
the night by the boys.
Flashlight/night,
lofting and sinking, we make
these exultations of oars.
We're always close to flying.
We always plan to fly.

CATCHING TURTLES

The slightest drip of a paddle
is too much. Let the canoe slide
by itself into the rushes and lily pads.
Lean far over the bow, your arm
a dead stick, drifting its shadow
through the water.
                    You scoop
a turtle from behind, snatch it
from the log, a hard bulge
escaped inward.
                    Snappers, you grab between
your careful fingers, arched
across the shell, back from
their craning dinosaur necks,
their mute bird beaks.
                    When you miss, you hear
the soft blip. Bubbles trail off
in deep, iridescent angles.

You don't catch them
for any reason. They scratch around
the canoe's wet bottom, leaving
stinking pools, and you bring them
two miles home. For days they wallow
and scrape their brown helmets
in the aluminum tub by the dock.
You add mussel shells and a petosky
stone for company. You feed them
worms, grubs, and a granddaddy long-legs.
You get used to hearing them.
When you go to swim, or sit
at the end of the dock feeding
the clamoring swans at sunset,
you start believing that skidding
and shukking against the tub
          is their real voice.
But when you let them go,
they ease down the rocks and slide
unruffled and heavy as fishing lead
under the alien weeds
in righteous silence.

THE CATCH

He calls her out of bed
to see them whole:
two sea trout, tails flaring
stiff over the tub;
two flounder, black eyes
skewed to the light;
and one muscular bluefish.

He says he hates the old roles,
but still he thunders
through the house,
his prize catch
the winner or nothing.
She pads to the sink,
files the sharpest knife
to a raw point, scatters
the two cats whining at the screen.

Then she sees him, crouched outside
in the single bulb, subdued.
He sets each fish's symmetry
on the plywood board
and drives the distasteful blade
behind the fin
into its wet heart.

Scales and entrails slide
across the board. He watches them
spangle in the light
as he digs the cavities clean.
He hands her the flesh,
sorry for its raggedness,
glad to be free of it.

He spreads his hands
like specimens
heavy with blood,
asks to come in again,
asks her to hold the door
because of his hands.
He has gone too far from need
to be forgiven—
almost as far as art—
but still he likes the hook
and the whole space under the sea
swimming with chance.

FISHING WITH BLOOD

They have waited for us in the country,
keeping the catfish fed,
brush-hogging the pond banks clear.

We must pull up a chair on the long porch
while they hold down Sunday afternoon,
circling their voices on episodes.

Then we can take the cane poles
from against the chimney
to find what is left of luck.

Small bream toy with the ball of blood
on the hook, so when the big cat
strikes, it is more than I am

ready for, driving my line down.
The great ache of the pole quivers
toward heaven, before the line snaps.

For hours we watch the cork bob
and dive, raising clues.
We wade to our necks for it.

We cast a flounder rig, its hooks
vicious in the pond. It claws the cork,
thrashes fourteen pounds of catfish

against the bank. The line snaps again.
We take the gift of our fish tale
in the pink evening up to the porch.

They draw it to them like a prodigal son,
full of flaws, but redeemable.
They go to work on it.

CHICKEN WILLIE

On Sweetwater Road, honeysuckle eats everything,
swims dark up the pines and down red clay ditches.
It moves on where the gravel turns to dirt, chewed
and gullied. A mile down, what used to be The Juke
buckles under the jaws of the honeysuckle.
A dozen years ago, you couldn't find a spot
in the yard to park on Saturday night, all
the white men coming to dance with colored gals.

The last years Chicken Willie Britt ran The Juke,
he kept Siller, his colored woman, in back. He'd sit
on the porch in his squat whiteness, issuing his stores
of Lincoln County's bootleg with grunts and nods.
The stuff rolled in from Tallulah, over the Vicksburg
bridge and down to the woods, where he kept it
on the move, buried, exhumed, buried. His two
men brought the bottles up, clammy from the dark.
You could say one pint or two, and Willie's snap
would call it up, a glint beneath the fist.

If you let the honeysuckle take you down
to the end of Sweetwater Road, you found
Chicken Willie's pond, a black brew draped
with willow trees, dripping bugs and larvae
into the gray mouths of Willie's catfish,
burbling up fat among the cottonmouths.

The left fork reached blacktop, then a couple
of miles to Willie's mamma's. Since the killing,
if you want to fish in Willie's pond, you have
to hear her story first. She rolls it out like psalms,
her eyes glazed, her fingers snapping beans:
          "Willie's daddy was a smart man,
built The Juke on the county line. When
the Lincoln County sheriff come, Daddy shoved
his chair across to Kopiah County, so all
they ever got him for was stealin' chickens.
Y'know he died at Parchman Prison, fifth time
up for chickens. Then my sons was all I had.

"Pat my middle son was walkin' Highway 20
on a spring drunk, when a log truck run him
down in the dark. But Leonard, my youngest,
always looked after his momma and his cows.
He stuttered some, but Leonard was a comfort.

"At election time, the Kopiah County constable
got nervous, since he'd promised to shut The Juke
down. He gathered up his men. Leonard
was takin' Willie some catfish I just fried,
and saw 'em all waitin' at the fork. So Willie
and Leonard took the pickup, to run 'em off.
I been down to the courthouse, the law they never
get the story true. They say Willie asked
the constable what he was doin', smellin' round
his property. Constable said he jus' wanted to talk.
Say Willie went for a gun under the seat.
All I know is the constable's men was in
the honeysuckle, and gunned both my boys
in the back, Willie and my Leonard.
Blood stayed on the ground till it rained.

"Well, that's all my menfolk, y'know.
That sonabitchin' constable killed 'em.
Say they gonna investigate! You think
anything come of that? Nothin' come
of that. Leonard never had nothin'
to do with that whisky. And Willie
never had no gun under the seat.
You can talk to Siller. She's back over
to her old place. 'Git me a pistol and I'll
blow their brains out,' she always tells me.

"—Honey, you can fish in Willie's pond,
but it's been eat up by honeysuckle,
and you'll have to fight your way in."

By the pond, The Juke leans into the trees.
Tendrils writhe through the dance floor; vines
flatten their suckers on the windowframes,
wearing the edges to sweet green. Lizards
green as leaves fly in and out the door.

38

APALACHEE BAY

The oystermen of Apalachee Bay stand
in their small boats. They spread their tongs
down from the boats, biting down bubbles.

The oystermen do blind men's work, rocked
in the visible cup of land. From the shallow
deep they dredge the green-black rocks,
scatter them over the trays, throw out
the halves and sand-filled wastes.
The oystermen cheerfully curse and rake
again under their shaken reflections.
In the keeper bins, the knotted clusters
clamp their wet mouths shut.

Up the docks, five women stand all day
at their five stalls under the windows,
shouting over the whistling saws that grind
open the oysters of Apalachee Bay.
The women's surgical fingers flick brine
and gather muscle. Through the glass
the women watch their men in the boats
come nosing in, shuffling the water's sky.

Below the legs of the women, five chutes
open to the bay, heaping shells black,
greenish, bleached, translucent, out
of their sight. The men rumbling up
from the docks with their wheelbarrows
eye the size of the heaps for a sure thing
against the vague roll of the sea.

At the windows, the women's eyes are sharp
for quality, measuring gift and giver, the slits
of their eyes more telling than their mouths.

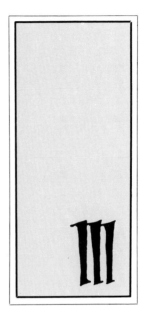

MAINTENANCE

Last Sunday when we installed the faucet
and cracked the sink, I knew
that nothing, however sound, is fixed.
Then the cat got sick and died,
and now under the bushes
where the white tail used to whip
there are only shadows blowing.

We make long walks in the dark.
Between streetlights, bent down
in our scarves, we take the cold air
against us like medicine, leaving
signs for anyone to follow—
our tissue breaking down, hormones
pulling back. At home,
the pipe under the sink still drips
from three joints where we've wrenched
the threads half bare; the refrigerator
has maybe two years left.
The mortgage is dwindling.
We accumulate frightening sums.

THE SCHOLAR'S CAT

I've never seen anyone take to a cat
the way you have. Six stillborn litters
she's had, and you keep hoping she'll give over

one fuzzy live one, one mewing paddypaw.
For such a growler, you are easy to this
fragile cat, who sits in the street,

mindless, who goes out and struts back
two days later, black tail puffed
from some night vision, or some Tom.

She shadows under the sofa, tail twitching,
scratches on the bedroom door at eight,
begs expensive food, whines and slithers

in constant heat. You stumble through
your days, insomniac, shoving at your own
bounds, and there she is, curled

and purring. Her spring fur flies
away like dandelion shafts. Your spring
hair grows long, curls out from your ears.

You don't shave for days. Huge raccoon circles
spread under your eyes. You read
yourself vague. But at three, when you've

long ago kissed me and every wriggling,
talking thing asleep, out of the night sky,
Zang! That cat hits the screen like a bat,

splayed, claws into every nerve. You lumber
to the door and let her in respectfully.
She curls in your lamplight. She is, for you,

the simple purr of nature's simple engine.
She sleeps when her eyes shut, she eats
when her stomach fusses, she makes love

when some blind itch shoves her, startled,
out the door. If her skinny self
concocted reproductions, the whole

sweet song would circle back around
and leave you pleased as punch
that nature knows so blooming much.

KEEPING FIT

Ten times around the tennis courts we jog
these three clay squares in the dark
when all the players have gone home

with their curves and bleached arms.
We count the laps and win our brief control.
We had been talking before, as we crossed

the field, the lantern wavering the gulleys.
I agreed that when you died, I would
send you South, beside your father,

both of you funnymen taking your irreverent
time in the weedy plot, mowed up against
the dark pines of your kin. You'd arrive

on a train among rumbling voices
of real men and real work. I can't
think of it: you must send me, instead,

off in a burst, a pyre to scatter its stars
according to superstition, or the habit of love.
Better to turn invisible. The elements

make poor signs of what we mean: your arm,
spreading sweat across my shoulder, my hands,
rubbing the knot rising in your calf.

Swans, North Eastern Island

Through binoculars, the swans stretch and flap
silent and distant as amoebae under glass,

not like gods, who feel their every gesture
hostage to a lonely universe, but indifferently

alert in this only marsh, this only inlet
in the world. They slide through beauty

too close to call it that. From this observation
platform, beauty's glossy, overwrought, the flat bay

hazed to one blue with the sky, marshgrass
moving like a single thought, seashore mallow

massively pink. It's lovely here, we'll say
later, meaning it opened up in us again that

longing for the picture taken, for desire's end.
I watch the swans for almost an hour, dizzy

from the slight waver of the lens. They take
both water and air with a white plunge,

equally at home. It is widgeon grass they want—
short blades, a breath long, the shudder

of the throat, the momentary ease. They seem
no farther than you are from me, and as beautiful.

HABITATIONS

SEEDS

A nest of boxes for my birthday—tin—
a pillbox painted with a butterfly,
one larger, shells, one flowers, one rimmed
with strawberries: four you've packed inside
a cannister, "Mandeville and King,
Superior Flower Seeds." How far some shapes
reach up the throats of other shapes! To link
their hollows like a wish? Or to scrape
together genus, species—cells already
grown? Give me a tin, I'll wish anything
fitting. I am no nomad. We're steadily
buying this house in the suburbs. We have paintings
on the walls. I have lost interest
in why this, not some other, is my address.

GODS

Something inside your body has led to these
conclusions, in the liver, in the enzymes.
Computers star the abnormalities.
You are chiefly materials, a lifetime
of dogged atoms, wrong. You make mistakes
or heal the ones already made—Who knows?
You test your waist, your chest, for news. You take
any word your skin can tell, its mask devoted
to the bone. You thought if you were secret, you
were safe, but it means you don't know which you are,
sinner, or sinned against: An eagle chews
your blackened liver—or you are an eagle, barbed
for flesh. Oh, love, the gods and heroes you used
to know have turned to you like children, confused.

SIGNS

The map had clearly shown a lighthouse x-ed
on Turkey Point. We climbed the stones around
the tip of the peninsula. The breath
of the Chesapeake reeled in and waves ploughed
straight to shore, dredged clues—old tires and plastic
jugs against the cliff. Beyond every wreck
of driftwood, every bend, you thought at last
the tower would be confirmed, but nothing stretched
above the kudzu vines.
                              "Are we sure
about the map?" I asked. "What good's a light
no one can find?"
                              You always could be lured
by hopelessness. You struck out as if there might
yet be some course to turn the drunken boats
toward dignity, and you the anxious host.

FIRE AND BLOOD

You can't get well. I close down, hypnotized
by smallness. Over me the pines rise dark,
the thought of darkness, otherworldly, wise.
Down here, faint moss, bright ferns, my insular
despair, a space scooped cleanly from desire.
—Not even here. A raspberry sews on
its own buttons—involuntary fires
break out, desire in every echelon.

A person climbs inside to hear herself
hum in the blood, where she is happier.
Then everything is correspondences:
Some bird throws notes away, leans off its shelf
and trusts the air. The tight earth breaks. Lacquered
stems rise past their knowing. Each cell balances.

SAVING A LIFE

You keep your illness, examining
its vague and shifty facets
like a jeweler as we take our daily walk.
By Thanksgiving, clouds and drizzle set in
and someone wants to die
on the railroad tracks.
Innocently, we circle the station,
into revolving lights that wheel up
one after the other, official vehicles,
raising a static of news.
The police are not going to let anybody die.
They are fingers of a hand across
all tracks, their voices surgically calm
in the night. The man is either drunk or drunk
with misery, throwing his reasons against them:
his grandfather dead, his little cousin
dead, his wife fucking some other man,
hey man, he yells down the dark,
there's nobody left.
Reasons enough, the cops should say,
nodding their heads. What the train can do
to him is hardly anything, we think.
Go ahead, we don't blame you, we want
to yell. We think he might take his grief
in his arms like a rock, then,
and roll away just in time, weak kneed,
but owning the trouble himself.
Safer, they talk him to submission,
his wife arriving barefoot in the cold.
They lead him to the cars like a prisoner,
dividing his suffering among them
until each piece seems like nothing,
until he is too poor to argue.

Bed-Buffaloes, Nose-Fairies, Car-Key Gnomes

This year the *Challenger* spread seven lives
against the dome of possibilities;
our country raided Tripoli. We watch
the televised melee like troops blast-dazed—
and I am living with you every day
alert and numb, inclined to love in shifts.
I try to think the larger world can keep
a truer course—of millions, some can fail,
or turn to stone. But in this room you are
my final scheme, gray-haired result; I
am guilty, bellicose. This is all we have
to send to space, contaminated goods.
The air here smells of chemicals and paint.
It jars our nerves; I'm convinced we've scarred
our bronchioles and closed synapses meant
to spark us into love. A Libyan child
surprised by flying glass is fixed against
the screen while Roger Mudd explains, but I've seen
enough sincerity to make me think
the biggest lies are best. The copper beech
uncurls again this spring as if the world
will last, and you and I have started this
book of cartoons our son brought home. We laugh
and laugh: bed-buffaloes, nose-fairies,
car-key gnomes. This is our home, our life.
For this much mercy, we can tell some lies.

THE HUDDLE CLUB

Three musicians up from the bottom
of a sleepless night, white-faced,
slack-lipped, counting up the losses
in four-beat country again.
The guitarist does not move,
his purple butterfly tie
loses hope at his throat.

Sometimes I walk in on the edge of what I know,
an arrow sings two inches from my ear.

At the table, the little man with probably
his wife, a woman maybe fifty with fat thighs
and heavy shoulders. When they get up to dance,
she hulks over him, billowing her arms over,
hips ballooning. Crouched, matching her face
with his hollow cheek, she heaves circles,
gathers red targets of light off the floor.

Their feet are a kind of air, pure
arch between love and work. I can see
he leads, his tight little legs
like bowstrings, pulling up
the band's nasal thud, pursing it
with a twist of his flat hips,
swinging it off, one knee down,
rest, cross, then stop.
His big woman knows his shapes with liquid
surprising grace. They are having a good time,
up to their knees in heartbeats.
They pass by me close enough to touch.

RABBITS

Saturdays, he drove in from his partly burned-out
trailer west of Clifty. I caught the memory of fire
in his hair and shirt, and the faint animality,
which I later knew as rabbits.
He was learning to waste nothing of what God gave him,
eating even the cores of small, bitter apples
he gathered in the fields. He hauled water
from the creek in gallon pickle jars.
His wife couldn't wait for his promise of better, since
he seemed content with his rabbits and Revised Standard
Version. Often, he said, she would call him gently to bed
but he stayed by the lamp, praying against lust.
Maybe she left because of that, he said.
Man is born to trouble, as the sparks fly upward.
He came back in his truck from buying rabbit feed
to find her gone with her clothes and the radio.
The people at church tried to fix him up
with various Christian women, but when he brought
his father, the retired preacher, to meet each one,
the cold light of God's will stopped them in their tracks.
Before I met his father, we had one long afternoon
hiking the fields. Two donkeys ate grass from our hands.
From the rises, we could see ten miles across the Ozarks
with the mist lowering against the summer trees.
Moved by this, he kissed me over and over
with a kind of fluttering regularity. Then we went
back to the rabbits hunkering in their cages. He sacrificed
one with a quick blade and skinned it like undressing a baby.
He wrapped it in a brown bag and gave it to me,
its forlorn life already soaking the paper.
I kept its terrible body in my freezer like a stone.
It was six months before I threw it out.

DEVIL'S DEN

For Barbara

We think we will get to the bottom of things.
We let the rock take us narrowly, one
at a time, against our backs, against
our feet, bracing us down the damp walls
into the dark. It is all angles, winging
thin and cold from the flashlight,
from the one clean leap of light
ahead of our feet. What comes next stands
granite. The earth is certain to hold,
balanced against itself for our lifetime,
our children's lifetime.

But in two hours we get to where
the rock clamps too tight to go on.
Whoever holds the light shuts it off
long enough to let the real dark press
our eyes and float us into its idiot lips.
Every absence is terrible.

So coming up from the dark
is delicate, reversed like a mirror,
and gathering implications. Each rock
has forgotten us, and will forget us.
It is enough to hope for a complex life:
leaves, dragonflies, impossible arguments
between two married people,
old women at bus stops, confused.
We take each other's hands
for balance. We sing "Born to Lose,"
and "Blueberry Hill," the way people do,
to let the sun know where they are.

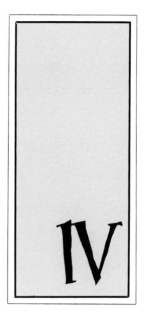

HE GIVES ME SOME IDEA
OF WHY HE IS THE WAY HE IS

1

Jaycee Park is where Wayman Fuller hid
in the bushes to waylay the coloreds who ducked
through at night on their way home
to the Quarters. (That was 1958 in Jackson,
Mississippi, language like a coin worn
faceless.) Across Bailie Avenue
is Virgil Street. It humps up, held then
at the top by four white houses, square
as books, with attached garages, hung
with wrenches, screwdrivers, pliers
on pegs. But from there the lean
began to roll and pitch, down
to the far end of Virgil Street. Beyond that
was only City Creek, the wide sewer
where the Baptist Church quit.

2

Five houses up on our side lived Lucky Cade,
pale as ashes. I loved him like a brother,
but he sold his bones to queers,
slow cruising, quiet, from Bailie Avenue.
His mother had black shoe polish hair
and an old man. And this is true:
they spooned poison in the oatmeal,
fed it to his grandbabies. She got off,
but he was electrocuted.
Daddy went to watch. You could do that
then. I remember he came home,
set his teeth on the edge of the sink
and threw up. Mrs. Cade's next man Snooky
stacked boxes at Liberty Grocery Mart.
Snooky had a hand wrapped
with a white towel, soaked with sweat
and ringed in salt. They went dancing
Saturday nights, in spite of that hand.

3

The house next to the creek
belonged to Mr. Thigpen, before he died.
That's where the oak tree was,
with the wisteria, a mother of a tree,
dark, dripping with vines,
lacing black over the dirt yard.
In the spring, purple swelled
like a bruise, awesome. In back,
Mr. Thigpen had thirty-five fig trees
which he paid me to pick. Early,
just before the sun, my gloved hands
held the finest bulbs, just ripe
and sharp, from the birds
that sailed and pecked at first light.
I hired me six coloreds at half-price
plus a sack of figs we set outside
the fence, and I kept the difference.
Everybody was happy, except
Mr. Thigpen, when he saw those
chocolate boys in his trees
among the fruit, rescuing it
from blacker fate.

4

When he died, the Sullivans moved in.
(That wisteria crashed blooms
against the porch, spring
after spring.) Saturdays, his momma
made me and Robert Earl Sullivan
shell peas in the front room. One day
his daddy barged in, glued the hungry
shine of his drunk eyes
on Robert Earl, and raked his paw
down a cheek. Robert Earl pumped
a fist into his teeth. The cracks
between filled with red.
My breath dropped below the shells
of peas. The sofa leg shoved
through the floor; the shotgun
went off through the roof.
When the cops came, Mr. Sullivan
asked them in for ice tea.
Corn bread, peas, and tea,
that's all they ever ate.

5

Grandma Sullivan had a boyfriend.
When he went away, there was a string
of them after that. It was glorious
when she came to stay. She would get drunk
and play the piano, and sing hymns.
Robert Earl and Tommy Dale and me,
fixed for a dance in our polished white shoes
and white shirts, had to stand
lined up for her to admire
at the piano. Fine young bucks,
she would say. When we came home
at three, she would still
be singing, "I Couldn't Hear Nobody Pray."
By then, the five-year-old was drunk,
too, on beer tea.

6

All of us had gardens. In the spring,
the only mule left in town brought heaps of manure
from somewhere, and the smell was rich
and thick, of living things packed down
cooking the soil, charming onions, tomatoes,
squash, corn and beans out of the dark.

PLAIN PEOPLE

GROSSDAWDY

All he wants is to drive his black buggy quietly across
the traffic, attracting as little attention as possible,
but his beard rages in the breeze, announcing him
like a prophet. His black garb is intended to make him
invisible as night, to let infinity show through,
but these days, infinity's occult. Cars slow down.
He could be an illustration of the billboard over him:
"Genuine Working Amish Farm. See Their Animals. Pump. Well.
Clothing. Guided Tours." He tries to turn his face
from the world, but he must look to his nervous horse. So.
If he stands still, convinced, wires and motors come
to wrap him in their longings. He is man-of-the-world
enough, gray-bearded from its brushing against him.
There is plenty to say, but he won't. A man speaks more
plainly from his bones, and beyond that, the earth speaks
for him, a cappella: the farms, the real ones, bearing.

FOR STEADY

A girl and a boy in a wide field, not holding hands,
holding elaborate stalks of goldenrod. They talk earnestly
as married people, but he is yet clean-shaven.
His black hat falls as he tilts to point out Canada geese,
honking and flapping to keep their huge V, to draft
the easier air. From below, they seem solid black.
The girl and boy are centuries old, old as cows and birds.
They wear black so surely, it is no color at all to them,
like skin. They look for delicate gradations (Eskimos have
a hundred names for snow). Their love hunts nuance,
clothed in flesh, which must clothe all the wishes of God.
But they hear the flesh say *arm, leg, breast* as boldly
as livestock, who make no errors of conscience, so
it is hard to think the world is delicate.
When he marries, he will never cut his beard again.
And she will pack up her wedding apron to be buried in.

TRAVELERS

The travelers stop at a crossroads where four farms
dominate the fields, three-generation farms with silos,
like a movie of someone's beginnings. The travelers
are listening to a rented tape that dispels myth and tells
the truth about the farms. They learn that a blue door
is merely decoration, and does not signal a marriageable
daughter within. They are told the grossdawdy house replaces
social security. They feel foolish, brought to church
after a long absence. Up the hill an old man in black
peers out of an outhouse, closes the door, peers out again,
a cuckoo out of a clock. He comes all the way out,
adjusting his suspenders, and shuffles across the road.
He turns back as if remembering something, goes back
into the outhouse, shuts the door. The body
is complicated, self-absorbed, and that is the truth.
It is housed in clapboard or stone, to bridge the gap
from earth to sky. It emerges, sometimes, silly,
half-blinded by the sun. Then every doorstep seems to
enter a cathedral. A lower, darker welcoming, a dignity.

THE OLD JEW ON HIS SLOW BICYCLE

The old Jew on his slow bicycle
pedals to the store, blind
to the tulip trees shattering
their gospel along the curb,
blind to the yellow cat rolling
in a gutter against the sun.
Every day, along some nearby street,
the creeping bicycle comes,
the olive coat, the brown beret,
the determined legs circling the air.

I have no heart:
I make him always the same,
pedaling and blind, but even detained
in these lines, he finds a way through,
a floater in the eye, sliding loose
from the focal point. He is far ahead,
with his brown bag. He is balanced
on the edge, while I am eaten up
by the sun, the trees, my direct
apprehension of the yellow cat.

GOAT

On the mound number 37 twists his foot
grinding the fat blue-shirted umpire with his fat orange face
into the acrid dust of the night field.
Sly. The umpire is sly.
Number 37 pitches the ball down a straight alley
and it slides, slides like glass
past the batter who does not move,
who wraps his arm across his face like a snake, still.
The sly orange face calls it. Ball.
Like round silver in a pinball machine,
the disgrace of number 37 pings against base,
base, sinking into the stands with a shining
clunk.
The batter trots to first.
Number 37 sees the sly eyes of the umpire
hot behind his mask.
The next batter leans to the umpire, leans.
The pitch slips by, pops off a board behind the plate,
plops in the spare grass.
Ball.
The pitch flies at the batter, and he jumps,
heaving in his stomach like an insult.
Ball.
The pitch guns off the fingers, sliding.
Ball.
The pitch is deflected by a transparent shield only 37 can see.
The batter walks.
Like clacking dominoes, the runners shift bases.

Number 37 reads the signs.
Knowledge rushes like blood to his head.
The diamond narrows, and there is only the funnel to the bat.
The planets splay unseen outward and arrange themselves
according to magic schemes.
Like numbers, the plan unfolds.

37 wipes his cap across the sweat drooling
into his left eye, and shoves it back fiercely,
triumphantly, over goat-like tufts of hair.
The spell of the umpire is weak, pale, and his sly smile
does not dare to move, now.
The pitch is straight and true and righteous.
37 knows that this is no wild pitch.
He does not flinch when the umpire calls
Ball.
37 bows his head like a priest.
The signs bounce from the hot glow of car lights behind left field
to the pale child wiggling high in the bleachers.
Only the umpire knows them all, and he plans and plans.
He sends secret passionate signals to all the rest.
37 is Old Maid, he signals. 37 is the eight-ball.
37 is queen of spades. 37 is Jesus.

Amy Lowell's Imagism

Amy Lowell walks
among the orange lilies that knew her mother
as well as her, and will know
no other Lowell after her.
With her cane, she supports her bulk
as if it were the collected weight
of all those Harvard men,
those Lowells.
In her garden at Sevenels
she is searching for her lover
after a day's work,
striding the cadence of a poem
among blue larkspur and peonies
definite and bright as the moon.
She is searching for Ada's silver heart,
the circle of her arms,
hard and personal
as *vers libre*.
"Double-bearing," she calls herself
and Sappho, and E. Browning, and E. Dickinson,
her sisters, with matrices in body and brain,
loving reflections of themselves
or making up reflections to love.

I am in my own garden
snapping off the withered suns of marigolds,
watering the silverdust,
thinking of Amy Lowell loving a woman
bodily, with her big body,
her writing the flute-notes of that love
into japonica and hedgerow,
unable in her time
to give its real source away.
I don't know any better than she:
a god of some sort
is planted in my torso.
My lips and breasts are flowers and moons.
My belly with its stretch marks
is another moon, scattered
with the prints of a fox's paws:
Once there was a mythological fox
who yearned for the moon
until he broke from the Virgin's grasp,
left dark, secret splotches
on the luminous disk—
All desire's displaced and out-of-hand.
I am a graven image, a supreme sight
on the black earth, as Sappho says.

EMILY DICKINSON'S LOVE

This is why you hear the spasm in my verse:
I am in danger. The butcher's boy brings in

the red slabs. He pedals through yawning streets
where shops rise yeasty along the banks.

Here, even the stair's toothed grin curls
toward my room. Downstairs, eddies of guests.

Against the turbulence, I put the vise to my words.
And lately, a new calm—someone I love!

For someone, I fold my hair and sit in patient
white, immaculately worded, expecting the bare sun

unveiled. It is dark. Outside my window,
frogs harumph for love, and crickets blither.

You cannot imagine my love's abyss of possible
names. I am pruning, finding the one,

although I know the stairs stand guard between us.
My love is a stake on the polished floor below.

Softly, I close my door, straining to hear his whistle,
his cordial refrain, to press it to my sheet

like a rose, its dizzy whorl stain
against the white. You know the spasm

in my verse? The dash against the word?
The closet room, furnished with codes?

O'KEEFFE

SHE LEARNS TO WALK

Years later, Georgia claimed
she remembered exactly
the quilt she lay on
in Sun Prairie, Wisconsin,
before she could walk, its
red stars and white flowers,
her Aunt Winnie's flowered
dress and golden hair.
Light rose to her fingers
from the half-dreams
of childhood, and sank,
the way dreams do
on waking. An ache, a vague
joy is left, and Rorschach
shapes riding the cusp
of what one takes to be
real, the material world or
the dream, depending
on one's education.

The assignment was to sketch
from a plaster cast of a baby's
hand. The sister
at the convent school wanted
it larger, like a sign,
and light as an angel lifting
up to God. Even then,
Georgia understood in
her black heart the
subversion required for art.
She made everything
bigger than it should be
and temporarily delicate.

SHE LEARNS TO TALK

She put influences away, began
her life again on hands
and knees with charcoal and rough
paper, rubbing shapes until
her body ached, a lunatic, working
into her own, unknown. By June
she needed blue: for two
thin flames, one a cocked
elbow, Georgia exact, a flute's
height and edge, hungry as jazz,
little stomachs of blue pulled
into the rise. She lived, then,
entirely in her body, her blue
blood breathing no air but
rising like mercury out of her will.

        "At last, a woman
on paper!" Stieglitz said in
New York when he hung her
raw intentions where
Rodin, Picasso, Cézanne had been.
        "But Stieglitz," a critic said,
"all these pictures say is 'I want
to have a baby.'"
        "That's fine," Stieglitz replied.
"A woman has painted a picture
that says she wants to have a baby."

In Palo Duro Canyon, Georgia saw
long lines of cows, made them blood-
red eggs, raising yellow dust between
two mountains' bones:
her nightmare of falling in.
Then she painted the evening
star six times. Its vacant center
broadcast yellow, orange, red, what
happens when you look too long, until
one star gives the sky
its meaning. The star is not
what you see, but the rash result
of it. The star slips back from
your memory, and is lost, or free.

69

A New Yorker Visits Her Exhibition

A man in a brown vest
observes jack-in-the-pulpits, painted
over and over, closer and
closer to the swelled
spike, the slit
of light. The trumpet flower
pillowed white toward its yawning
shaft. The sunflower spread
like a whore for the
bees. Georgia sits bolt upright in
the corner, enduring his
plod and gawk. Her hands lock
their secrets around
each other. She turns
her flowers loose. If this
man had been the one who stuck their seeds
into the soil, they would go on
without him, or die
of weeds, no matter, growing
again in wilder transformations. He
stands before Georgia's monstrous
calla lilies, hands
in his pockets. Perhaps he has almost
discovered his small
importance in this process, and has
begun to look into his heart for
another point of view. She
watches the symmetry
of his limbs as they turn and
return almost against their will to
the same vaginal tease: a star, a bell-
shaped cry, "Come in, come in!"

She Marries the Photographer

Stieglitz

I focus on her thigh, the wings
of her eyebrows. She is so lean
the film can't find her, but
finds her messages, which
she has made to look like
herself. Posing makes her itch.

70

O'Keeffe

Stieglitz talks all the time,
drawing the line of his thoughts
around his friends. Lord!
I want my gallery white
and curtainless, the colors
exactly where they should be.

Stieglitz

Every angle of her, variously
exposed, a dozen tries
in my darkroom; but she, too, paints
the same barn five times.
Against great odds, our children
stick to the paper like art.

O'Keeffe

When we sweep the relatives out,
Lake George blackens and steams
toward winter; I can paint nude
in my shanty. Stieglitz walks down
for mail from New York, his black
cape flapping like a crow for news.

Stieglitz

So now she needs the West.
Its bald light dissolves me
from her consciousness. All is new.
She paints bones six months a year.
In late fall, she comes to me
from the badlands, brazen with canvases.

O'Keeffe

The telegraph boy flags me down
in Abiquiu. By the time
I fly East, there is nothing to do
but rip the pink satin lining
from his coffin and sit all night
sewing plain white linen in.

AN EXPERT EXPLAINS HER WORK

Anything pared to the bone
needs interpretation, so
no one will be bored. You can't
say look there, and there. Only
here, like a devotional.
Once, Georgia O'Keeffe stole
an immaculate black river-stone
from a friend's table with no
explanation, and she
is well-known to have painted
that same shape in a number of
excuses: the single alligator pear,
the sunflower's eye,
the obdurate moon,
the hole in the pelvis bone. How
far it is to eternity, and how
little we have to go on! Stripped
of flesh, the pelvis bone
is capable of flying
open like a camera lens.

Then she was forever
painting, like a curse, versions
of the door in the patio wall
at Abiquiu. It took her ten
years to buy that house, that
door which had once been
sold for two cows, a bushel of
corn, and a serape. Still, it made
no apologies, a rectangular
door in a patio wall,
sharpened and scrupulous,
a place on the wall to
let your eyes
stop and collect their forces.
If anything went in or out, you
could see, and put a stop
to it, or be the only one
waiting, thus, the most beautiful.

LOVE, FOR INSTANCE

Love, for instance, is a set-up.
Like in Chagall's painting, *The Birthday,*
you would think every object in the room broke loose
by spontaneous combustion. But love has been planned
to happen this way for some time, although
this occasion is new. When her lover was thinking
flowers, you must know he figured hormones
and could already imagine the wings of her collar,
her breasts like wings, Mary Poppins, transported,
unmoored. And look at her eyes as she kisses him,
wide open, deliberate as his flowers. She watches him
roll out of her mouth like a ghostly language
and drift down her back, *en train.*
She has made him up.
You know she has made him up because he has no arms
and can't even be a real lover in that condition,
rubber-necked and armless.
He couldn't even hold down a job.
How wonderful it is to get things into that condition,
to make even the paisley print on the wall wiggle
like tadpoles! It is especially a good idea
since outside one window, a row of guardhouses
plods whitely down the street, and outside the other,
nothing but a ladder of more windows.
With love, you can have a red floor, and rise above it.
But don't expect to be believed, entirely:
The melon, the cake and the stool are round-eyed,
but it is a feigned innocence, not surprise.
The blunt knife is aimed at the hole in the cake,
a little joke. The bulging purse lies on the edge
of the table where it might fall to somebody's ruin.
The clincher is the stool, absolutely round
and black, bouncing off its legs, a hole
you fall into just under the flowers.

EDWARD HOPPER'S WOMAN

There is Hopper's woman.
She stands naked
looking out the huge window,
flooded with godawful light,
her thighs muscular, taut and white.
She has no place to go,
and her jaw is squared.
Her red mouth
tells very little in the way of stories,
her lips smeary, stifled
and worn.
Beside the cloister-like bed
she stands perfectly still.
She will never go anywhere,
her black high heeled shoes
carefully fallen beside the bed.
Her lax stomach leans forward.

The thighs—
they are not even hers,
like a cry escaped and not
belonging anywhere.
They bulge heavy, just hiding
the crotch of the silhouette.
It's like the only secret Hopper knew
in that sunlight,
how she could leap
out into anywhere if she chose,
but she stands quite willing
and not quite sure
to let the brush
paint her down.

Photo by Fletcher Chambers

Fleda Brown Jackson's poetry has appeared in *Kenyon Review, Iowa Review, Poetry Northwest, Ariel, Southern Humanities Review,* and other journals. She teaches English at the University of Delaware, where she edits *Caesura,* the university's literary magazine. She has published essays on William Dean Howells, as well as on D. H. Lawrence and other contemporary British writers. She is coeditor, with Dennis Jackson, of *Critical Essays on D. H. Lawrence,* published by G. K. Hall and Company, and past editor of *The Newsletter of the D. H. Lawrence Society of North America.* She was the recipient of the 1987 Delaware Arts Council Individual Artists Fellowship.

More poetry from Purdue

All That, So Simple
Neil Myers

" . . .*a tribute to the power that rhythm and a sense of language-as-music can give poetry.*"—James Moore

"*[He] writes with such artistry that whatever he presents us with appears in its essence.*"—Arturo Vivante

72 pages, illustrated, ISBN 0–911198–56–3, $4.00

The Artist and the Crow
Dan Stryk

"*[His] poems are grounded in his effortless and strict voice. And his voice is an eye. . . . a fine and welcome collection.*"—William Heyen

"*A reader finds landscapes or settings, and their inhabitants, that come alive in richly textured but unvaryingly precise language.*"—Ralph J. Mills, Jr.

96 pages, illustrated, ISBN 0–911198–71–7, $5.25

A Season of Loss
Jim Barnes

"*[He] moves with assurance from the past to the present, linking them firmly in his vision and helping his readers be authentic in thought and feeling.*"—William Stafford

" . . .*simply fine. . . . Clarity of vision, clarity of voice. It is a privilege to read such a good poet.*"—Fred Chappell

80 pages, illustrated, ISBN 0–911198–75–X, $5.50

The Spine
Michael Spence

" . . .*a strong, clear collection. Its spare imagery is absolutely appropriate for the human and natural landscapes it evokes with both economy and grace.*"—Joseph Bruchac

"*The collection has an overpowering sense of geography.*"
—Colleen J. McElroy

76 pages, illustrated, ISBN 0–911198–89–X, $5.75